The Coffee Bible

By Danae L. Samms

Illustrated By Ariel McGowan

This is for someone who is truly amazing. Someone who always has our back. Our idol, our best friend, the one we love most in the world: our coffé

PSONNETS

I

I have found life from your rising hot steam,
Without you I would move like a dumb slug.
I would prefer you to almost a dream,
Oh sweet real life is you inside my mug.

I love the sound when lids open pip-pop,
And the smell of fine brown soft coffee grounds.
There will never come a day I shall stop,
For life without you is worse than it sounds.

Not once in life will I touch caffeine free.
Any day without caffeine be a quagmire.
Oh, no other place I would rather be
Than filling my dried soul with your strong fire.

Without you by my side I cannot think.
Dearest coffee, you are the best to drink.

II

I have traveled all around the wide world,
Just check my Instagram pictures with notes.
Each place is remembered in my cupboard
I have more collectors fun mugs than most.

I hardly use the one brought from Cancun,
Because "hand wash only" is annoying.
A colorful story goes with each one
I think coffee with me is not boring.

We can drink some homemade Starbucks coffee.
In the Disney mug you'll want to borrow
I'll fill my mug with cream of a toffee,
And talk for hours about Monticello.

I could use each mug more often than naught,
It's just Han Solo is the best I've got.

III

You fool; mistake be made, I hate this fad,
I do not think, I know it tastes like piss.
Certainly the worstest coffee I had;
My mind will not be changed on this.

Please hold my cup so I may slap your face,
Forcing the barista for hours to make.
A plain, black cup of joe would win that race,
And does better keeping us all awake.

Honey, I do not care what you may think
Of my thoughts on something so trivial.
It smells asparagus and looks like ink
Sold from the store of a sad, failing mall.

If there's one thing I hate, it is cold-brew,
Ariel is with me, she hates it too!

IV

In life, many a man has come and gone,
Because my standards are much higher than
A lot of girls my age. I've not done wrong.
I will just be picky because I can.

My mom always told me, listen and share,
"The only thing worse than being alone,
Is wishing that you were." Trust me, my dear.
Only one never made me cry or moan.

Every morning I beg he stay a while,
Hold him and spoon, breathe deep, feel warm, and sigh.
Coffee is true the love who makes me smile.
Unlike past men, he shall not tell a lie.

This love, my coffee, makes a promise true
He says, "I will never abandon you!"

V

whir-crunch whir-crunch whir-crunch whir-crunch whir-crunch
whir-crunch whir-crunch whir-crunch whir-crunch whir-crunch
whir-crunch whir-crunch whir-crunch whir-crunch whir-crunch
whir-crunch whir-crunch whir-crunch whir-crunch whir-crunch

whir-crunch whir-crunch whir-crunch whir-crunch whir-crunch
whir-crunch whir-crunch whir-crunch whir-crunch whir-crunch
whir-crunch whir-crunch whir-crunch whir-crunch whir-crunch
whir-crunch whir-crunch whir-crunch whir-crunch whir-crunch

whir-crunch whir-crunch whir-crunch whir-crunch whir-crunch
whir-crunch whir-crunch whir-crunch whir-crunch whir-crunch
whir-crunch whir-crunch whir-crunch whir-crunch whir-crunch
whir-crunch whir-crunch whir-crunch whir-crunch whir-crunch

Each day I wake to a stern reminder
That I must invent a silent coffee grinder

VI

Today I long to hold the one I see.
Tomorrow I will want him that I feel
Lightens my soul and draws nearer to me
Sweet dreams of lavender and purposed zeal.

My tender heart split in love shared by two
Sweet souls whose charm will both bring me delight.
Infatuation comes by each when true
Happiness is found by either in sight.

One is the sun while the other the moon,
One sweet flowers other beautiful snow;
All inspire a melodious tune
That puts our love on display in show.

No choice between the two will come from me,
For I equally love coffee and tea.

VII

Who was the first one to take pause and think
Of keeping that bit from the morning pot?
Mixing sugar and cream brought forth new drink
Remade to please basic bitches a lot.

While most would toss that old coffee toward
The sink, instead someone made something nice.
Overcome by frugal spirit they poured
Old coffee on a fresh batch of cold ice.

The charm of fresh cup of Joe is quite gone;
Replaced with sweet drunk fit for late summer.
An iced coffee is much better than none,
Because no coffee is a real bummer.

While not my favorite one through and through,
It is so much better than cold brew.

VIII

I'd like to see a Parisian Cafe
Where I can drink coffee by a blue sky.
I'd sit and be that guest in a beret
Looking toward the Seine as boats float by.

How strong is coffee made on open fire
Built exploring plains or a mountain range?
Both made for life that does not require
The luxury of comfort or sweet change.

Be it from walk ups on a busy street
Where with travel our interest did pique.
Despite any last barrier to greet
Coffees a language we all speak

Across this world, though sea or land I roam,
The best coffee always will be from home.

IX

Quiet. Simple mornings undisturbed by
Work or requirement find my bed and
Body melted into one lullaby.
To arise I have not any demand.

Ask not how long I have lingered in sheets
Bearing thread count higher than my budget.
Budge not will I though light through blinds does seep.
Only one prize will I take leave to get.

Farewell to warm! Across the cold wood floor
Into kitchen where sweet coffee awaits.
Despite unrest displease not this quick chore
To fill a mug much larger than my face.

After journey to the kitchen for it,
Return to bed and with my cup I sit.

X

Mornings delight me not despite the day
That waits ahead be good or bad or blah.
More sleep may come but I am not okay
Enough to leave covers and fetch a bra.

Never let pride prevent you from asking
For help from the good bean inside that cup.
Without that juice my life would be lacking
The will to leave home or even wake up.

Cast off blanket, old pajamas and sleep;
Struck now endless of possibilities.
One cup brings on a full new day to reap
In life, love, or responsibilities.

Anxiety take the helm on cup three;
Cup four, cup five, no one ever stop me!

XI

Relentless the afternoon make burden
Any task we may long or hate to do.
Tired forbade that we may get word in
During any problem old or anew

We long to answer the call of sweet sleep
It seems in desperation our one hope.
Slumber at desk the solution to keep
Going upward in this endless work slope

Fall prey not yet to complete exhaustion
Brought on by inescapable work load.
If coffee be the food of life pour on.
Give me excess of it; that caffeine mode.

And now that slump of day be quite reversed
All work complete from the coffee coerced.

HAIKUS

I'm not an addict, you're just mean

Can't get enough of
A soy peppermint mocha
Every December

3:00pm

Just the thought makes me
Feel better on the worst day
Get in my belly

Secret to Happiness

Get yourself a cat
Then pour a cup of coffee
Honestly, that's it

Best Friends

Wrapped in a blanket
In a seat by the window
Just me and coffee

True Love

A cup of coffee,
Strong and sweet, is like a hug
When you need it most

At Home Artisan

So many flavors
So little time to drink them
I just love coffee

Hazelnut and cream
Fresh ground Columbian
Death before decaf

Smooth French Vanilla
Drop of Italian creme
I'll never drink black

Top it with whipped cream
Throw calories to the wind
Life is short, drink sweet

True American

Sometimes I'll drink tea
Only when I feel British
Coffee everyday

Drink what God Intended

If I were a car
You would be my gasoline
Glad you taste better

Haiku 9

In truth, the best friends
Are the ones who stay silent
And warm in the mug

Savage

I don't understand
How someone is happy with
Just one black coffee

Haiku II

Lattes know how you feel
Mochas make your life brighter
My Cappuccino

Saturday Vibes

My usual seat
Unlimited free refills
Panera is love

We all Have a Problem

Everyone loves the
Bean juice with such devoted
Infatuation

Morning

Freshly ground each day
Colombian coffee is
My favorite kind

Haiku 15

The quick pick me up
If coffee is my kind of
Afternoon delight

Love

His kisses are sweet
His hugs both warm and tender
Coffee, not a man

Haiku 17

I'm not that picky
I like my men like I like
Coffee; strong and sweet

SIMPLE DESIGNS, SIMPLE PLEASURES, COFFEE

THE COFFEE BIBLE

FREE VERSE

I Love You

I love you.
Sometimes it's hard to say
I've never been more certain it's true
You're on my mind night and day

I love you.
You light my withered fire
If you ran out, what would I do?
Every morning it's the same desire

I love you.
Begin each day with you beside me
Blonde roast, cappuccino, or simple home brew
My love, my heart, my coffee

Hope

I see your sleepy eyes
But it's not time to quit
Hope is closer than you realize
We have to stick to it

In the kitchen, the break room,
Or the shop around the corner
Help will be here soon
You won't be tired forever

Coffee Cannibal

People enjoy
        Me
        All over the world
        I
Help them with
  their morning
        I
        Keep them awake
          on the late shift
            They seek
                My
                Servings after
                  a heavy meal
            But...
          I am never able
        To enjoy,
         To seek
          To use
            To drink
              Myself.

-Ariel

Sugar & Cream

A strong cup says, "good morning."
A decaf says, "good night."
Sugar and cream keep pouring
Until the taste is right
Only an idiot would offer me
One regular, black coffee

Coming Home to You

Travel makes me weary
Roads roll on forever
Even sunshine feels dreary

I miss your taste
I want to hold you
Journey feels like such a waste

Despite the distance
Through crappy shops
I will remain persistent

Passing days won't keep me blue
Because my coffee,
I'm coming home to you

THE COFFEE BIBLE

THE BOOK OF
GRANDE

I

In my mornings I call for coffee. We cannot begin with less than sixteen ounces. The small may only have need for a tall, but the strong begin with grande. My heart calls out daily for standard portion. Be it filled of my mug at home, or a stop on the way of my morning, it will be there. It awakens my soul. My spirit. I rise. My bones find life. With each sip my purpose rises higher and higher. If sweet coffee were to leave my life, existence would cease. All ambition would collapse and fall away.

A day without grande is a day of turmoil. Despair would fill me. Exhaustion would encompass me. The world would drain me. I would collapse and fall victim to the snare of a caffeine headache. Shackles of sleep would enslave me.

I cannot be left alone. Without a medium coffee I am a hopeless wanderer. I would be lost in the forest of fatigue. Uncertainty would incircle me. Sleep would ensnare me. My desk would only be used for naps. Like wounded doe I would stumble.

Without the aid of coffee, the evil of tired, the hunter, would find me. Tired would track my steps and overcome me. Be it glade or forest or office or driving a car, the arrow of sleep would pierce me, and I would succumb to its relentless will. Like a flower on the cusp of autumn, I would wilt and die. I would be trodden down to the dirt.

Time would forget me and all my deeds. Any use or aid I once could offer would be lost. No work would be done. Projects would fall and decay. Bosses would rot. I would fade away as all reason for life slipped away like sand between fingertips.

Yet with a grande in my hand I rise. Be it hot or iced, homemade or store bought, Starbucks or Dunkin, with a grande in my hand I will find nothing but victory. No longer would I walk with the crutch of caffeinated tea. For the world lays before me, ready to conquer when I carry a grande.

II

Let each of us take up a cup. Drink and be filled. There is neither sweet nor black, alcoholic or specialty, homemade or bought, for you are all one in your love of coffee.

It is with coffee that we prevail! No longer would life fade away. No longer would color escape and time slip by like a worthless whisper. For with our coffee we will rise.

Grande wraps around us like armor. With coffee we break through the morning victorious. Exhaustion falls away. Any trace of tired flees. Like a mighty warrior we stand caffeinated. Take up your grande and live to fight another day.

Work flows like a steady river. Projects and meetings tug like a swift current. Deadlines are boulders and cliffs threatening to shatter and break us. But coffee is a bridge of life. With it we are lifted above the waters. On it we cross without worry. Though work roars below us, we stay dry. Too long we struggled on the raft of afternoon naps. Now we are untouched by the waters of work and worry.

With coffee we are made strong. It's presence in our mugs gives hope to a wretched life. The caffeine that flows through our bloods gives us strength to fight. With coffee we are made strong. Drinking coffee makes us a new person.

Without coffee we are nothing. Life is an impossible race with each new day. Why then would any man "cut back on caffeine"? Cast aside these friends that know nothing of health. They are not friends. They have been blinded by the deception of fools on the internet. They will wilt away with the sleepy.

Drink coffee and be merry with life. Allow yourself the joy of a grande every new day, and all will be well. Coffee is not an affliction, but an aid to health. Our livers are cleared. Our hearts are given life. Above all, our soul is made happy.

III

With every sip, I don't just feel like I can be someone else, I know that I can be someone else. I feel myself emerging to become the best version of myself. We are carried forward to a better tomorrow and a better self. Let all the old, faded parts of this human fall away.

I leave them in the night. Now they are behind me, I am a new person. With a coffee in hand and a brew in my soul I arise as a phoenix from the ashes, reborn to a new day. Let my life start afresh with the coffee in my hand.

The presence of coffee in my body and life bring me to a higher level. From now I will not lie with the dead or stumble with the weary; I will fly with caffeinated. I am not sleepy, I am awake. Awake with coffee.

No longer will the weight of exhaustion oppress me. No longer will the early morning and Monday drag me down. The tired has been ceased with your sip. I am a slave of weariness no more. With a mug in my hand their shackles have been broken. Coffee has wrapped me in its arms and drawn me into a better day.

THE COFFEE BIBLE

IT'S NOT GOOD FOR COFFEE TO BE ALONE

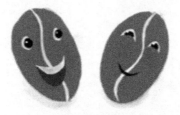

THE BOOK OF BEANS

I

From the bean it began.

Behold I was a slave to the tired. I was enchained by sleepiness. I knew no relief but the nap. Then, coffee was with me. After one cup I was a new creation. Its mercies make me new each morning. To the regular first then also to the decaf.

It grew as a bean for me. The bean was plucked and ground for my heart. The brew was slow roasted for my soul. Before cream and sugar, I knew coffee would give me strength.

Strength to drive and strength to work. Strength to live and strength to love. After coffee I can drive through tired. I can work though the job sucks. I can love the stupid. I can do all the work days with the strength of coffee in me.

Your presence in my mug warms my hands each morning. Though the night be long, the thought of you at the end gives me hope. I will not fall into the snares of the sleepy when you are with me. You bring hope with each dreary morning, encouragement to the endless afternoon, and comfort to the late-night project.

Lead me not into decaf carafe but deliver me from exhaustion. Brothers and sisters be warned, humans are weak, and mistakes are often made. Do not always trust the signs. Be it a meeting or breakfast bar, though it says "regular" and the other "decaf" they could be reversed.

That is when you should simply ask. Or if no one is around, drink two cups. I tell you it is better to have two cups of coffee and need to pee than one cup and it be decaf.

A decaf's place is in the home, not in the

workplace. Decaf should only arise after dinner when nothing but sitting and sleep lay ahead of you. Though he is sweet decaf is frail. Decaf cannot carry you through the day. It is better that he should remain in the kitchen, within a cabinet. Only use him after a dinner party, and even then, only at request.

II

The rattle of the beans in the bag is a joyous melody. The roar of the grinder is a symphony. The steam and flow of the brew is a lullaby. This mastery of beans is for you and me. The songs they sing are for all who love coffee. For we all find a comfort in their presence.

Buy them ground or grind them yourself. Or perhaps eat them whole, coated in chocolate. They are the foundation of energy and the beginnings of coffee.

Without beans there is no coffee, and without coffee there is no life.

THE BOOK OF MUGS

The swirl of the spoon, the mug in my hands, the caffeine in my heart. Where would I be without you? You deserve a vessel of the finest porcelain or biodegradable material. Though the mugs be pretty, they are honored to carry coffee.

Every new journey brings me another mug. Memories from travels warms my heart as coffee warms my soul. There is no such thing as too many commemorative mugs. They remind us of friends and travel and the coffee that brought us through.

Coffee has a way of turning up when you need it like an old friend. Traveling is made better. An unfamiliar place is much less frightening with the smell of coffee brewing. Local stops on road trips and shops in airports feel like high fives that keep us going. Though the coffee be not sweet like home, it's like a smile and an act of kindness from a stranger.

Nights in a strange bed can be long and restless. Despite the unfamiliarity of the kitchen, the smell of coffee makes it feel like home.

We call it joe because it's like an old friend.

THE COFFEE BIBLE

A PICTURE MAY BE WORTH A THOUSAND WORDS, BUT WHAT'S WRONG WITH A FEW MORE?

Coffee dribbling
across
the white tablecloth
I'm in trouble
now...

Coffee steam rising
such splendid shapes it creates
I sit and daydream

THE BOOK OF JOE

I

Where would we be without them? The morning rush, the afternoon lull, and the light night pick me up are all made better by the love the baristas give.

Am I lazy to be enjoying their craft? Certainly not! Hard work can be met with the occasional treat. My treat is the coffee that I did not brew myself but was brewed for me in love. For baristas so loved the world that they gave their only begotten drink. That whoever partakes in it shall not tire but have everlasting energy.

II

Though the baristas dearly care for our drink and its flavor, an evil lurks at their side. Be watchful for her, nitro or no. Many has she deceived and brought to ruin. She is the sushi of the coffee world.

She is an ever-present wickedness. She lies in deceit and fills many a glass. Countless have fallen prey to her pull and lure. She sits on the counter every day and sings to the coffee lover. "Drink me!" she calls. "I am sweet to the taste and kind to the teeth. Look at my style and color. Fill your Instagram with my beauty." She is a deceitful mistress. Her presence in your cup will bring nothing but heartache and despair. Run far from her temptation. Do not listen to her songs.

The path of the cold brew is vanity that leads only to destruction. She whispers to the coffee drinker, calls to the barista. "My drink is sweet and my glass fulfilling." But from the beginning she was astray. She is a brew made in the shadows and only for deceit. Her cup is untrue. Her drink is error. Do not fall for her wicked pride. Be ever watchful! She beautiful to the eye and cunning in her glass. Stay away from the cold brew mistress.

While she seems a delight her presence on your tongue is like a mouthful of horse piss. Her brewer thinks of no one but himself, and casts aside all wisdom and wellbeing. He is a fool that is far from the path of coffee. Oh, coffee drinker beware! Be ever watchful of the cold brew and her chilling ways. Though she looks a beauty, she is poison in a jar. All who take her drink are slaves of vanity and victim of iniquity. Fill your belly with the wisdom of iced coffee and flee the cold brew's snare.

Lead me not to your folly! Be gone tasteless bean juice! The cold brew is wicked and a destroyer of taste buds!

III

In the shadows of the night I was afraid. The shout of an alarm left me drained. I faced the morning alone and worn. Yet the hope of coffee was there. The path to the kitchen is dark and full of terrors. Without the promise of coffee, I would be lost to exhaustion forever. The sputter of the maker is more beautiful than a thousand songs. The smell of your grounds is sweeter than a valley of lilies. The steam from the pot draws me close like a mother's hug. Without you in my mug, I am frail. If you are not in my life I am fatigued and finished.

AS MUCH COLOR AS ARIEL WAS COMFORTABLE USING

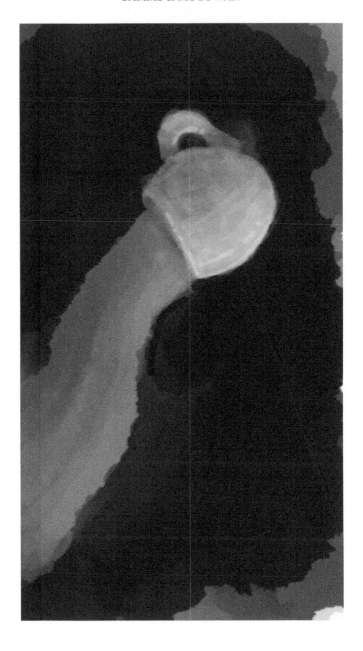

THE COFFEE BIBLE

ABOUT THE AUTHOR

Danae L. Samms is an enthusiastic creator. Her writing began when she was four with her first play, and continued to grow to a degree in journalism, a blog, and the novel *September Christmas* (available on Amazon). Regularly, she keeps up with a blog of unqualified advice on writing and everything else. The only thing she's been doing longer than writing is horseback riding. While horse shoes were never her forte, Danae has spent plenty of time riding and training. Most of that is with her horse Maggie.

danaelsamms.com
facebook.com/dlsamms
Instagram @dnays

ABOUT THE ILLUSTRATOR

Ariel began creating at a young age with bright crayons and colored pencils. She soon discovered she preferred a graphite-and-ink world devoid of such radiance. The Coffee Bible illustrations are her first work with actual color. Ariel currently lives somewhere between Narnia and Antarctica with her leprechaun husband and three scale-babies. They are her muses and the loves of her life.

Instagram @ijustcreate

40851674R00046

Made in the USA
Middletown, DE
01 April 2019